Little People, BIG DREAMS®
STEPHEN HAWKING

Written by
Maria Isabel Sánchez Vegara

Illustrated by
Matt Hunt

Frances Lincoln
Children's Books

Little Stephen was born in Oxford, England, just as
a great world war was raging. At night, he would look
up at the stars and wonder what else was out there.

His parents loved science, as did Stephen and his three siblings. They all ate dinner with a knife, a fork, and the company of a good book.

Stephen was never top of the class, but at school everyone called him 'Einstein', like the famous scientist. One day, he built a computer from clock parts and an old telephone.

Curiosity always came before schoolwork with Stephen. But still, he made it into the best universities in England: Oxford and Cambridge. He wanted to solve the mysteries of the universe.

Stephen was busy enjoying himself studying cosmology, when suddenly…

… he started dropping things and tripping over for no reason. Even his speech became hard to understand.

Doctors told him that a rare disease was paralyzing his body and he had only two more years to live. Stephen felt like the whole universe was falling down around him…

Instead of looking down at his feet, Stephen decided to look up at the stars. Maybe he couldn't control his body, but in order to study the universe, all he needed was his mind.

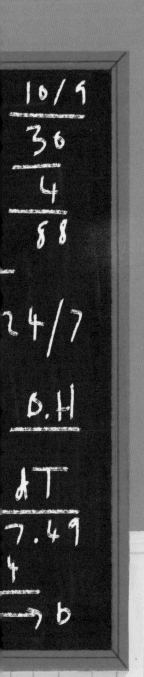

His wife Jane stood by his side and gave him all the support he needed. They had three children and Stephen loved to give them rides on his wheelchair.

Stephen turned his attention to black holes, some of the strangest and most powerful objects in the galaxy. So powerful, that not even light could escape from them. Or so scientists thought...

But Stephen proved that black holes were not so black after all. There was a tiny light escaping from them. It was named 'Hawking radiation'.

By this time, Stephen had lost his voice and found a new one with a robotic drawl. With his new voice, he dictated a book that helped the world understand the meaning of the universe.

Stephen believed that one day, humans would cross galaxies to live on faraway planets. He celebrated his 65th birthday by taking a zero gravity ride with a team of astronauts, leaving his wheelchair for the first time in 40 years.

By becoming the most brilliant scientist of today,
little Stephen made an amazing discovery:

"however difficult life may seem, there is always something that you can do and succeed at".

STEPHEN HAWKING

(Born 1942 • Died 2018)

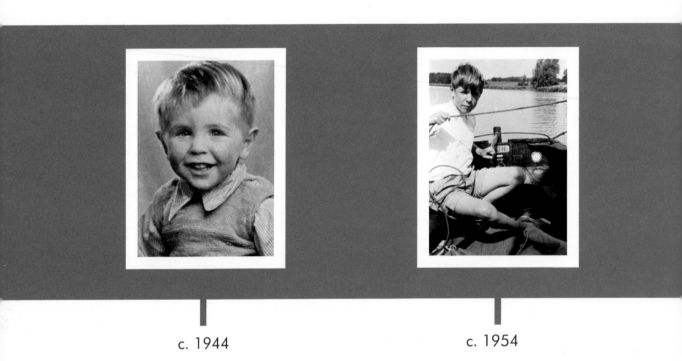

c. 1944

c. 1954

Stephen Hawking was born on 8th January 1942 – exactly 300 years after the death of the astronomer, Galileo. Stephen had an eccentric upbringing in a household of thinkers. Their family car was an old London taxi, his parents kept bees in the basement, and they made fireworks in the greenhouse. From an early age, Stephen used to lie out in the garden, stare up at the stars, and wonder how the universe worked. But at school, he was not an exceptional student. He was always more curious about activities outside of class, like making computers and solving his own equations. Despite this, Stephen's brilliant mind took him to Oxford University to study physics, aged 17. It was during his time at Oxford that Stephen started to become clumsy. He didn't think about it too much, and carried on studying, eventually graduating with a first-class degree.

1962

2008

It was when Stephen moved to Cambridge University that he received a diagnosis of motor neurone disease (ALS). At the age of 21, he was told he only had a few years to live. Stephen threw himself into studying with a new focus. He finished his PhD at Cambridge University, and later, became an esteemed professor of mathematics there. Then, whilst researching and writing, Stephen came up with his black hole theory. He showed that matter can escape from black holes in the form of radiation. He called it 'Hawking radiation'. This changed the way the world thought about the universe. Stephen lived until the age of 76, proving his doctors wrong. He continued to study the universe, write best-selling books, and give public speeches until he died. Stephen is remembered as a brilliant physicist who sent shockwaves through the world of modern science.

Want to find out more about **Stephen Hawking?**
Have a read of these great books:

George's Secret Key to the Universe by Stephen Hawking and Lucy Hawking

All About Stephen Hawking by Chris Edwards and Amber Calderon

A Brief History Of Time: From the Big Bang to Black Holes by Stephen Hawking
(advanced reading)

Brimming with creative inspiration, how-to projects, and useful information to enrich your everyday life, Quarto Knows is a favourite destination for those pursuing their interests and passions. Visit our site and dig deeper with our books into your area of interest: Quarto Creates, Quarto Cooks, Quarto Homes, Quarto Lives, Quarto Drives, Quarto Explores, Quarto Gifts, or Quarto Kids.

First Published in the UK in 2019 by Frances Lincoln Children's Books, an imprint of The Quarto Group.
The Old Brewery, 6 Blundell Street, London N7 9BH, United Kingdom.
T (0)20 7700 6700 **www.QuartoKnows.com**
First Published in Spain in 2019 under the title Pequeño & Grande Stephen Hawking
by Alba Editorial, s.l.u., Baixada de Sant Miquel, 1, 08002 Barcelona www.albaeditorial.es
All rights reserved.

A catalogue record for this book is available from the British Library.
ISBN 978-1-78603-732-9
The illustrations were created with digital techniques.
Set in Futura BT.

Published by Rachel Williams • Designed by Karissa Santos
Edited by Katy Flint • Production by Jenny Cundill

Manufactured in Guangdong, China CC072021

12

Photographic acknowledgements (pages 28-29, from left to right) 1. Young Stephen Hawking, c. 1944 © SWNS.com 2. 12-year-old Stephen Hawking, c. 1954 © SWNS.com 3. Stephen Hawking graduation from Oxford University, c. 1962 © SWNS.com 4. Hawking Offers Case For Space Travel On NASA Anniversary, 2008 © Handout via Getty Images

Collect the *Little People*, **BIG DREAMS**® series:

FRIDA KAHLO	COCO CHANEL	MAYA ANGELOU	AMELIA EARHART	AGATHA CHRISTIE	MARIE CURIE	ROSA PARKS

AUDREY HEPBURN	EMMELINE PANKHURST	ELLA FITZGERALD	ADA LOVELACE	JANE AUSTEN	GEORGIA O'KEEFFE	HARRIET TUBMAN

ANNE FRANK	MOTHER TERESA	JOSEPHINE BAKER	L. M. MONTGOMERY	JANE GOODALL	SIMONE DE BEAUVOIR	MUHAMMAD ALI

STEPHEN HAWKING	MARIA MONTESSORI	VIVIENNE WESTWOOD	MAHATMA GANDHI	DAVID BOWIE	WILMA RUDOLPH	DOLLY PARTON

BRUCE LEE	RUDOLF NUREYEV	ZAHA HADID	MARY SHELLEY	MARTIN LUTHER KING JR.	DAVID ATTENBOROUGH	ASTRID LINDGREN
			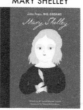			

EVONNE GOOLAGONG	BOB DYLAN	ALAN TURING	BILLIE JEAN KING	GRETA THUNBERG	JESSE OWENS	JEAN-MICHEL BASQUIAT

ARETHA FRANKLIN

CORAZON AQUINO

PELÉ

ERNEST SHACKLETON

STEVE JOBS

AYRTON SENNA

LOUISE BOURGEOIS

ELTON JOHN

JOHN LENNON

PRINCE

CHARLES DARWIN

CAPTAIN TOM MOORE

HANS CHRISTIAN ANDERSEN

STEVIE WONDER

MEGAN RAPINOE

MARY ANNING

MALALA YOUSAFZAI

ANDY WARHOL

RUPAUL

MICHELLE OBAMA

MINDY KALING

IRIS APFEL

ROSALIND FRANKLIN

RUTH BADER GINSBURG

MARILYN MONROE

KAMALA HARRIS

ALBERT EINSTEIN

CHARLES DICKENS

YOKO ONO

ACTIVITY BOOKS

STICKER ACTIVITY BOOK

COLOURING BOOK

LITTLE ME, BIG DREAMS JOURNAL

Discover more about the series at www.littlepeoplebigdreams.com